For Al[...]

with best w[...],

Peter.

SKY-RIDING

Sky-Riding

PETER BENNET

HARRY CHAMBERS/PETERLOO POETS

First published in 1984
by Harry Chambers/Peterloo Poets
Treovis Farm Cottage, Upton Cross, Liskeard, Cornwall PL14 5BQ

ISBN 0 905291 53 0

Printed in Great Britain by
Latimer Trend & Company Ltd, Plymouth

ACKNOWLEDGEMENTS are due to the editors of the following publications in which some of these poems have appeared: *The Honest Ulsterman, Iron, The Literary Review, Poetry Durham, Poetry Matters* and *Stand.*

'Aeromodellers' won a prize in the National Poetry Competition 1981 and has appeared in *Poetry Review* and in the Mandeville Press pamphlet *First Impressions.*

'Apfel Strudels in Elysium' won a prize in the Lancaster Literature Festival Poetry Competition 1982 and appeared in the Festival Publication *Poems '82.*

'The Silence' won a prize in the Sotheby's (Arvon) International Poetry Competition 1982 and has appeared in the *Sotheby's International Poetry Competition Anthology.*

'The Dwarf and the Battle Planes' appeared on the Morden Tower broadsheet *Poets for Peace.*

Paul Stangroom's drawing is one of a series which first appeared in the LYC Gallery publication *Wall.* It belongs to Roger Garfitt, by whose kind permission it is reproduced.

for Gillian, Alizon and Dominic

Contents

Light On The Wanney Crags

Warriors they are, and veterans
of long assaults; ·
scabbed by plots where sheep must crouch
to fret the unforgiving grass.
Their heads are emptied out by rain, their feet
abused by pitchfork-tossing pines.
Backs to the wall of sky
and stripped to grit, except
where mist or snow can compromise
their fierce nudity:
they can do nothing but resist.

Stone-shouldered and unkindly twins:
but I have seen their stacks
turned tractable by light,
and as the peaceful clouds unwind
each blown embattled height
is touched, and taught a mystery.

Then the crags stand in accord
with all whose battles are adjourned for joy:
and those, unlike the rock, who hold it fast
against a time when they may fall
among the kindnesses of light
infrequently, or not at all.

At The Three Kings

Less drama than expected—three small kings
upright, knee-deep in yellow turf,
and then a fourth, up-ended long ago.

The children round on us, appalled
by such reward for short-legged miles
through spruce plantations, then across the moor.

They are very old, we say, *Two hundred
lifetimes* must *be old*—but they
have not acquired a grasp of lifetimes,

only distance walked and hunger pangs.
They buried someone here, we say,
With treasures round him—look, between the stones—

of course, it's all filled up with earth since then.
They scramble, mellowing. *Is this the hole
they put him in? Can I get in there too?*

The sun shares final brightness of the day
with Dour Hill and Saughy Crag
and half-sized people in a lonely place.

And we—who have a grasp of lifetimes—see
how hunger fades in solemn play,
and how that ancient faculty persists.

For James, Katy and Carlos

10

Redundant Steelmen Learning To Draw

Annexed schoolroom full of men,
silence wrapping wide shoulders,
unspringing speech.

There are two tables; on one,
two shells, a plaster Benin head,
white and white.

On the other; a jug of wooden
spoons, an aubergine, an apple,
and a cloth.

Brown and brown. Steelmen drawing,
clumsy-cautious. Affirming strength
in risking it.

Hills fill our window. Sun-bathed
views are vast. Inside, each vision
narrow and acute.

Today we read 'Ozymandias';
prized the parallel. Look on Consett
Works, ye Mighty,

and despair. I was a lad
at this school, one man said. Now
I'm fifty-three.

What counts? What have we found out?
It's worthwhile work to try to draw
an aubergine.

Aeromodellers

The fells take on a texture
of chenille, darned with bitter grass
and creased by ancient diggings.
Light catches on a strand of distant
cattle, jet beads along a hem
of shade. Breakfasted, I wait
for them to come. Each Sunday
sees the same unfolding ritual.

On Green Rigg a car draws up,
another. More arrive until
a cluster grows. Then the business
of boot-lids, stretching limbs,
a trading of hellos. Boxes
are unpacked, model aircraft
lifted and displayed, pampered
into flight. Responsive to their

radios, bright wings perform
embroideries, over and again,
then butt the grass, discarded
by the air. This is when the sound
begins to needle. In winter
I don't feel the thin insistence
high above the growl of Lawson's
tractor. But in summer after

croissants, bought in town and heated
up by Calor Gas, we sprawl
and let resentment bloom for grown-
up boys with dwarfish expertise;
for evenings out of reach of common
sense, hunched in garages or lofts;
for nights consoled by *Aeromodeller*
with fingers nicked by Stanley-knives.

Yet nothing of mine amounts
to more than this, their refuge
from domestic blight: and how
can I begrudge to share this
place with them? Our title-deeds
are snowflakes on the hills, and all
the brightest clothing of our lives
is woven out of sunny afternoons.

Apfel Strudels In Elysium

Un boulevardier, c'est moi,
but quite content, sans boulevards,
in coffee shops
of smart department stores.
Particularly this one,
Tyrolean,
girt with cut-glass mountain peaks.
Between which dirndl girls
as neat as gingham flit,
decanting lakes and lakes of cream
from cartons with a happy cow.
Here we are already half-way up
the socio-economic alps.
There are no misfits
in the chatteries,
no Mrs Mopps —
the clientele at pasture by the coffee streams
is plump and rich and perfect.
From my corner by the wall
of fat gateaux
everyone looks good enough to eat.

A mannequin begins a trawl
for flatteries —
taller than the Matterhorn,
and surely naked as a cuckoo clock
beneath her avalanche of furs.
She twirls a smile and flicks
her price-tag specially for me.

When I'm inordinately old, and filled
with every necessary virtue,
Send such as she
to guide me from the nitty grits,
up to an Elysium
where apfel strudels bloom like asphodels,
and money yodels in the tills.

14

Oysters With My Stepfather

Tea, as always, so constrained
that ice encroaches from the buns,
across the arctic tablecloth
to rime the edges of our words,
and cool the tea-cups in our hands.
Yet we warm each other for an instant,
in a memory of Matlock Spa.

We took the bikes there once,
in thirty-odd, before the war.
I saw a lovely thing,
a floating hoister
on the water,
with its silver pearl . . .

Mispronunciation halts him:
but I feel affection curl,
past the ogre of my childhood,
to touch a cyclist from the pit-heaps,
far from home and ripe for marvels.
Then, as something in him answers,
son-et-lumière begins.
In Matlock, on the ink-black water,
all the bright regatta-boats
are oysters with their beaming pearls,
while here the warm spring evening chills.

Clock-Tower At Beamish Hall

Coal could raise a clock
to sit the slates just like a gentleman
bidding rusty afternoons
to collier's grandsons in the stableyard
refreshment room. Above the clock
the bell's gazebo: ten stained columns
lift the dome, cage the voice
which roused a hundred labourers,
bear the brunt of sooty rain
from worked-out coal towns and the coast
where all the money grew. A weathervane
is jostled by the sycamores.

So much remains,
foursquare forelocked craftsmen would be proud:
and those who hocked the light of day
to raise this gentleman might grin
to see the wreck of his utilities
measure to a jot
how much the times have changed.

Crazy Dog

Distance has dwindled him to running points:
his quick white dash, his smudge of black,
are accidents beneath the bulk of sky,
small movements in a weighted sack.

He risks a start, tail sprung with confidence,
but stops before a second passes,
supplicates, then tacks a reckless angle,
sheepdog-fashion, through the sheepless grasses.

There must be countless crazy ways
to be a crazy dog—shadow-poaching,
calling echoes from the moon—
this one sees the sky itself encroaching

on his liberty. The failing daylight strikes
no barriers which are not his alone:
a dog with half the world to run across,
who acts as though somebody pegged him down.

He'll find the road eventually, or else
his owners at their summer caravan
will stir themselves to fetch him home,
and lock him up so he feels free again.

Ancestors

They seemed to thrive among the hills,
the known if not the unknown ones,
saw barns and long grey houses made
at Radditch, Carr, and Castle Naze
and willed them on:
mounding an up-ended cairn
whose names and properties are stones.

I also climbed the Pennines' back
from which to add my own,
and bending forward to the rock
can catch their speech down half its length
splitting echoes of the name:
Benet, Bennet, Bennit, Benett,
like blessings from their windy farms.

For Michael

Cows

'Giddup—go on lad, take 'em down.'
Of course, he knew they had more sense
than I did, man and beast
conniving at the impudence

with which I strode and slid behind them—
slicing with my cowboy-stick
great loops and arcs in morning air
a safe length from the awful lick

their tongues might give, or dangerous tails—
then ran ahead to let them through
to pasture by the Leek Canal,
where I was not allowed to go.

For Gran

Bistro-Kitsch

Nothing is what it seems—and least of all
this rash of fruit hooked up across the wall

on real string. Oranges begin and end
the whole extravaganza: suspended

in between are pears with ochre bruises,
brash bananas turning up their noses,

fat apples, cherries, plums and then a bunch
of sea-green grapes. Enough to spoil your lunch

if they were genuine, but they are not.
Each week they take them down and drop the lot

in soapy water, hang them back to dry—
bistro-kitsch, a larder-full of trompe l'oeil.

The stuff does no one harm, and gives the joint
its ambience. But still, I'll make my point:

meretriciousness just makes me angry—
neither art nor food should leave us hungry.

No Damage

The place seems lonely, as it sometimes does,
despite the beasts in ambling residence
about the hill,
or meditatively sconced in grass.

We startle sheep on our way up,
bedraggled outriders among the bents
and lichened stones;
disperse a company of cows outside the gate.

But no one, nothing, in the garden;
our infant strawberries are safe in bed,
the shrubbery un-grazed,
our un-nipped nubs of rhubarb growing red.

Inside, a corridor of light
connects two brightnesses—a window-view,
a square of floor—
and gilds a wedge of mud from someone's shoe.

Three chairs, two sofas, tidily in place—
just one pushed back, its tartan
rug askew. Over there
a cupboard door hangs quietly ajar.

Beside the hearth the fire-irons fly
their flags of shadow,
unperturbed, and taciturn
as when we touched them last, a week ago.

But look, not all is as it ought to be:
our lawn-mower has left a vacant space,
the Tilley lamp
has somehow flown from on the mantelpiece.

An acid blend of silences occurs,
and then a queasy clash of fact
with memory:
someone has been, and taken things, and hacked

the heart-wood from our tree of privacy.
                                    We know
a small part of his story, how he slept
out on the moorlands
in his car. Walls and furniture have kept

whatever detailed memories there are
of an unlucky man, on an unlucky day,
who brushed them—finding
things, pricing them, and taking them away.

Now the police have taken him—out of work,
it seems, perhaps a family to keep.
He did no damage: closed
our gate against the ever-hungry sheep.

Writers At Chisel Hill Mill

We left the cars to cool themselves
like hot loaves, ticking from the sun,
where spruced-up granite stables made
a nest of shadows; found a path
which led through shelving lawns to seats
beside a mellow wall (where thoughts,
already cast in sentences,
enriched the mist a sprinkler raised
in blond air spiked with faint bouquets
from grass-food pellets soaking down)
and basked there, adding words to words,
while summer laid,
on flags which mill-hands booted smooth,
its first entirely certain days.

And afterwards we toured the house.
The pool which used to shove the wheel
stood thick as toffee, barely stirred
by half a dozen Muscovies.
In neat rooms, heavy beams and cogs
were cleanly kept and purposeless.
Two carpets on a polished floor
declared that quiet millstones lay
beneath the clever noise we made.
I weighed an early harvest there,
as blunt folk from that valley would
who ground for bread
with stones which we had left unmoved,
and found my words were light as air.

For Sarah Banks and the Beamish Writers

Shittleheugh Pele

'The Durtree Burn ... winds through a narrow and craggy glen, at the
opening of which, on a point of dry and fertile ground, stands the old mansion
house of the Reeds of Shittleheugh ...' *Hodgson's History of Northumberland*

More welcome if you go alone:
the green straight vein was once a dike,
   stick close to it
   until you find
a single hawthorn, fully grown.
Enclose this in your arms for luck.

Now skirt the soft ground underfoot.
Head south, look for the gable-end,
   the broken strength
   of all the Reeds,
a tooth-house, hollow to its root,
forlornly tenanted by wind.

Their pint-sized fortress was a farm.
Peer out beneath the lintel. Search,
   perhaps it was
   a garden here
the hawthorn pip was stolen from,
round which your fingers will not reach.

For Ralph, Wol and Leon

24

Dry-Stone Worker, Sandysike

Though something jangles in his head,
a priest inside an empty church
might move like this:
his actions have the quiet truth
of rites observed in solitude.

The thin wire at his throat connects
headphones to his tranny:
blanks out the thumping of the wind,
the seep of water into ground
which will outlast him, sap his wall.

Passengers

Time condenses. It's not hard
to bring the subject into focus:
some pseudo-self disconsolate,
fog-bound as on a gas-lit station
circa nineteen fifty-three.
Loudspeakers in the vaulted ceiling
are gargling with cancelled journeys:
posters offer Scottish mountains,
formal gardens near the sea.

Passengers are soon recruited,
ticking through an iron turnstile.
Relatives and friends compose them:
my father shadowed in a trilby,
closest ones returning somehow
clustering along the platform
shaking hands and sharing gossip
underneath the slotted signboard
with its bin of destinations.

Then something like a train arriving
blackened by the coal it uses:
cold compartments empty, filled
with darkness from the tunnel,
some of which the crowd dispels.
Not hard ... but I don't see me board it,
even urged by loving voices:
the picture shifts each time to mountains,
formal gardens near the sea.

Crane

How loftily he balances
his long blue nose, a seagull's-hop
above his treasury—
his concrete jewel-chests of aggregate,
his rare menagerie of timber baulks.

Wellman Boyd of Annan built him—
chieftain of an ilk of cranes.
Tipsy, too, one foot on and one foot off
the harbour wall,
while foghorns of the fishing fleet
pipe his favourite lament.

Villa Real Café, Consett

High noon: a faked-up hacienda,
frontier kitchen down the trail
where heavy industry
has turned its nose towards the slump.

Artics have the place pinned down:
are breaking wind
an inch beyond the flimsy wall.
The door makes rapid pistol-fire.
The windows flinch.
A cab-top Michelin bandido
wipes the sunlight off my plate.

Men will eat surprising things:
two giants up before me in the queue
took apple pie and Tizer,
chips with gravy and a pint of milk.
Greasily kind-hearted girls
build breakfasts twenty hours a day.

El Patròn—moustaches like a Gaul—
slops the last gold from his mine. High noon:
the pot-holes slicken on the park,
but all these trucks are hauling scrap
from what remains of Consett Works.
When it's sold the town will close:
much bad hombres ride again.

The Silence

Traces can be found towards the lough
and soon I hold
a full-grown silence in my sights:

a lack of sound more elderly and grand
than all the pines and birches
whose water-edge I share. It rests

across the lap of water like a blade,
separating trees and sky
from their reflecting selves. Perhaps

my bench of driftwood cracks: the silence
listens, turns and starts.
The geese are up and walk towards me,

shorewards on a plank of light: clumsily
they raise unruly wings,
breaking out their syllables like hounds.

For Rosa Davis

Quinces

You might not even notice them
Look—the garden bares its ribs!
thinking they were tarnished leaves:
but there are seven quinces
on the smallest bush.

Shall we find how best to cook them,
the best way to eat quince,
or wait to see how winter leaves
burnished medals on the bush?
Look—the garden bares its ribs!

The Dwarf And The Battle-Planes

'A being of the latter class used in former days to haunt the extensive wastes that spread over the upper part of Northumberland, houseless, treeless and trackless.'
Tomlinson's Northumberland

They should be careful near our roof,
learning how to split the dusk
repeatedly, like ripping tripes.
Predatory sorts like these
may sometimes meet the moorland dwarf
whose riddles leave them scatterbrained
among the boulders and the bents.

Imagine, while a gloomy evening
dissipates the battle-planes,
the far-from-human stratagems
of someone old as Ottercops
who tricks them back towards the earth
and parachutes their pilots home
to practise harmless trades.

Our doubts expand beside the fire:
no heather-culled intelligence
could countermand the black machines
or mend their purposes,
yet in between the flame and shade
the dwarf keeps watch behind our eyes
and peace enfolds his parishes.

Digging For Moles

A cold March Sunday sprawls itself
across the fell's upholstery,
spilling sleet and snagging drystone seams
on broken fingernails of light.
The Landrover—a bucking crawly,
tacking for the firmer ground—
is braking every now and then,
nose-ditched or perched wry on the slope,
and Charlton, hunchbacked in the wind,
manoeuvring to start a cigarette
or tug his trousers open, piss
against a wheel.

Each time he stops he takes a spade,
jabs and skitters back the earth and leaves
molehills levelled,
tunnels booted-in and plugged
against the purblind animal's return—
or else the shovel-thrust of blood and sound
which lets the weather in.

Lottie Little And The Trees

Imagine her thin sticks up there—
Lottie Little—while she doled
her soup of rue and solitude
and slouched trees spat into the bowl.

Outside, the fell's cold vacancy
and inside, that intention rooting
deeper as each year drew in
to have them hacked and burned to nothing.

Imagine the elder by the gate—
which once purled sunlight to entangle
the taste of milk with greenery
for children grown while she stayed single—

cut down for what she heard it murmur.
And even then she could remember.

The Last Of Them

He was the last, a widower.
Douglas, his only child—my father—dead.
It's only recently that, looking back,
I think I know what sort of life he led.

Grinning dogs above the iron grate;
cold-water scullery, and the murky glass
at which he scraped his chin for fifty years,
oil-cloth on the table where he ate.

A photograph of Nellie when they wed;
himself, in war-time bandolier, and by the bed,
a florid parchment from the firm
to mark a lifetime in the parcel room.

Pink ham, celery and salt, his treat;
his pride and luxury a high coal fire.
His parlour open straight in off the street,
over-stuffed with lumpy furniture.

He was of the proud and decent poor,
unenvied and unenvying. Certain of his place
in life. Sure to welcome me, his nearest,
as out of cash and soaked in sooty rain,

I made a detour off the road from Manchester.
The last of them, and what was I to do,
when tugging up his bedroom sash, and half awake,
he called down, 'Douglas, is it you?'

Sculpture For The Flats

Unfocussed even while I look intently:
mud-bathed trolls, sub Henry Moore,
seem unfit to represent
such triumphing against the odds
as high-rise families contrive,
kindling the City Road
from curtained slots.
Perhaps these darklings are to blame
for what goes on each night in stairwells:
she whose head had been laid open
will stumble off to trawl the street,
the one whose fist indents her back
will drink the giro
and the block-like blunted child
will spray FUCK ART
in shining letters on their plinth.

Wildfowl

Mist-bound by the tarn as wildfowl pass,
rehearsing futures, editing the past.

But look—do wild birds lug their troubles home
or are they always to or from?

Resident in air while shifting through it—
do they plan the thing or simply do it?

This afternoon ideas as daft as that
are typical of me. From where I'm at

sky-riding would be fine, so trim, so bright,
within a thoughtlessly reshaping flight.

So how would it seem to stop being me
and climb through falling mist unconsciously?

Souvenir Of Malling

The iron-corseted Moselle,
in black, with bands of chilly light;
a burp and swash of barge-trains running
cargo out from Germany;
an onion-turret fussed by trees:

Although a year churns in between
that dawn and this, the goldcrest wren—
brisk, thrilling smallness, now, this morning,
flanked by ferns like greater wings—
can flit my distance to all these.

My son, reached soonest, winged by reeds,
as engines clubbing hard at water
fractured sleep and drew us down
to count the wealth, in shrouded tons,
dark with dew from Germany.

And turned me, not to have him share
my fear of strong means, dimly seen,
by which unwieldy laden hulls
slide through nights unceasingly,
like fathers following their sons.

Under The Floorboards

They found a full-grown Persian cat,
mummified between the joists.
A lunchbox, chewed by rust, contained
two fragile sandwiches, a cupcake,
hard as stone. Elsewhere, a cache of girls,
all pleated shorts and halter-bras,
spent forty years unthumbed
since someone met the real thing.

                                    I myself
surprised the skeleton of a mouse,
entire and delicate, whose nest
disclosed, in tiny scraps,
the news of fighting near El Alamein.

For Allan, Ian and Kevin

Sile Na Gig or Playmate Of The Month

I met her on a freezing morning
where the road clings to the lough.
She made three beckonings:
from a cow-pat near my feet to start with,
merely lifting amber knees,
the hardly-there-at-all chemise,
and sharpening her grin.

Farther on, between two heather-brakes,
naked this time, smudged by light,
the same insistent glossy shape,
each hand weighing out a breast,
nipples pertinently pricked,
hair in an entanglement,
elsewhere a tuft: her covert lip.

I turned for home, and there among the sheep
she sat again, attracting me
by shifting slightly in the wind.
She made her wide split-beaver, ancient M,
a finger at the opened curls:
held me, the only moorland beast
equipped to read her, stupidly enthralled.

The Sile Na Gig (often spelt Sheila Na Gig or Sheelagh Na Gig) is an ancient symbol consisting of a crouching, and assertively sexual, female figure. There is a famous example among the carvings in the Church of St Mary and St David at Kilpeck in Herefordshire. I have adopted the spelling used by Seamus Heaney.

Split-beaver is a term used by glamour photographers to refer to a pose in which both the vagina and the pubic hair are clearly shown.

Sunken Barges

Beside Mount Vernon Cottages
the cut breathes in to fit a bridge
and then breathes out expansively.
My grandfather remembered it
as working water: the turn-around
for moorings at the colliery staithes.

Six barges lodge out in the gut,
scuttled in their own reflections:
knees and elbows, mossy fists,
one fractured flank still visible
cluttered by the waterhens,
willows rooting where their cargoes were.

I met the village bombshell here,
just once. We hardly spoke and yet
she helped me play the hero, though perhaps
she only really liked to flirt:
a prize for both of us,
awarded by the Macclesfield Canal.

Things have changed. Someone runs
a down-at-heel marina.
Pleasure boats pop nervously
round water-gobbled hulks
which no one can afford to dredge.
She married locally but hasn't found

that middle-age amounts to much:
serves behind a grill-room bar, and wears
the brassy burnt-out look
of one whose girlish victories
lie swollen like the sunken barges,
far too difficult to budge.

Happiness Is Egg-Shaped

The world seems coded to exclude him,
egg-at-a-desk, homunculus:
and literature, all fallen leaves.

I focus him. Complete these sentences:
The speedway-rider ... boxer, astronaut,
pre-chewed pap,

rat-race primer,
fodder for a dismal norm.
Somehow we are joined in vision:

on the tundra of the page
ink comes crawling. His moon-face waits
for help, instruction, impetus.

Today he will not press himself
to read the clearest sign. Each coin,
each minted speculation,

holds the same flat value, valueless.
He barters for excusal,
offering his lunar grin. Soft rims

of helplessness preserve him,
rolled on spokes of vacancy.
I touch his shoulder, circulate.

Hare-brained literates are waiting,
fingering the loaded words.
The call him Happiness.

Barmaid

Floundering in her pool of faces,
with scarcely chance to scratch an itch,
she dips her head, gulps privacy,
bobs among the pin-up bitches'

buoyant bubs, as pink as scampi,
which bring strange fishes looming down.
Glances like the lips of lampreys
are lifting flesh on all her bones.

Despite her aches she twirls to serve
but thoughtlessly displays a thigh.
In frothy swirls the blunt snouts swerve
and every glass contains an eye.

Visiting

Our visitor decides to leave.
To see him go,
sheep throw off their camouflage.
The dimples of a Roman fort
reconvene on lower ground.

The fells themselves in stripping down
lift their elbows into spring
but nothing green is quickening:
trajections round the fruitful year
may miss this landscape utterly.

So rawness of old ground revealed
must speak for birth, unfolding, change:
while farther back towards the sky
the high hills still
lie clenched by snow, unvisited.

Funny Man

Good-looking, gloomy, awkward cuss:
he'd never dance.
But let somebody ask his wife . . .
You'd have some action from him then,
as edgy as a chisel-bag.

It was the fall that sorted him,
the whole height of the foundry crane:
surgery, six months in plaster,
surgery again.
Great pain unlocked a funny-man,
and when they came to wheel him home
he'd salvaged laughs from splintered bone
and friends for every foot he fell.

He sees the bright side nowadays:
finds life too short.
And dance? He'll get up when you like,
three-legged if you count the stick,
and twitch his boots and callipers.

The General

The khaki greatcoat makes it hard
to pick him out beside the wall,
gumboots planted in the ditch.
A sudden stoop may catch your eye,
the straightened back,
the shoulder tremor and the flap
of unhitched epaulettes.
His grandfather and father worked
along the same route, barked their hands
to link horizons with this heap
which fallen, chews with broken teeth
its mess of rain.

His left arm jumps and turns a stone—
lichen on the neb of which
has grown a quarter inch in width
since their stint ended—shifts
the anvil of his palm
to make rough cheek and hammer kiss
exactly for the trimming split
which fits it in.

Once walls are down you'd never tell
what held them up:
three months' work is mapped for him
in quarryings as clean as bread
which flank the ruin up the fell
and shrink into a little thing
the man whose knuckle-bruising knack
for teaching stones to toe the line
will put them upright and cajole
rubble into wall:
bind the narrow top with turves
to bed his stubborn soldiers on.

Old Man Watching Trains

A coal-train like a string of cradles
moves across King Edward Bridge:
clanging steel made gentle
by the distance and the dawn.
The brakeman looks towards him,
does not wave.

He feels the pull of years behind him,
heavy as the rusty cradles,
feels the incline in the morning,
the slow descent before the bridge.
The brakeman looks towards him,
does not wave.

Looking Through A Parched Sea Holly Bush

I see three things which bring me grief:
first, among the cross-toothed curls,
two pearly snails
anchored to a drying leaf;

then, how heat-clasped boulders sit,
each old when some first living thing
woke up to its journeying,
rubbing down again to grit;

and, farther out than I can reach,
how woman-like my daughter wades,
careless that her girlhood fades,
as sea takes home the sun-warmed beach.

Your Turn, Solomon

It could be Resurrection Day
behind St John's
but all the newly quickened dead,
their eyes closed under newspapers,
have slumped about to sun themselves
on tidy grass among the graves
and nothing moves, unless you count
peace-marchers wagging cardboard bombs
and pigeons nudging crumbs along
this table-top of Solomon's,
but no one seems to notice those
as cylinders of heat roll down
imprinting limbs,
in spite of pamphlets, mushroom clouds,
in crazy marks of unconcern
across their bed of rags and bones.

It's your turn, Solomon—unwrap
your parcel of integrity.
The times are still more difficult
than those in which you did not stoop,
in which your uncorrupted press
was hitched to truth and liberty.
Shake up the layered alphabet
and comment on this itch for death
which digs a pit
through blandly euphemistic lawns
and yawns and lolls beside the lip
in unexampled apathy.
Perhaps you have some points to raise
about irrationality,
or forthright speech, or politics
where nightmare rides diplomacy?

Our conscience goes to rest its feet
at some church hall. A sip of air
expends itself on city sweat
and bodies move,
turn fronts or backs towards the sun,
while, over-arching and aloof,
tall trees he was acquainted with
suspend fragilities of light
a stone's throw from the Printer's Pie.
There is no sound,
except for pigeons on his stone
still querulously questioning:
How many summers have there been
since Solomon took thirty-nine
and sank beneath his weight of prose?

How many summers still remain?

'Sacred to the memory of Solomon Hodgson, in times of unexampled
difficulty the honest and independent conductor of the *Newcastle Chronicle*. As
he could not stoop to court the smile of any man, so neither did he fear any
man's frown but, through the medium of an uncorrupted press, delighted in
disseminating the principles of rational liberty and eternal truth. Nor was he
less estimable in private life, in his affections ever awake to the best sympathies
of our nature. The manly vigour of his understanding found its equal only in
the kindness of his heart.'

(Inscription in the churchyard of St John the Baptist, Newcastle upon Tyne.)

Fête Day At Bellingham

I
Prevarication among coals:
the darkness loiters

lichen grips a thousand stones
each offered, quiet as a pulse.

Morning stalls, delays
acceptance of a moorland shape.

Curlews questioned me from sleep
to pass on news of this:

my hearth's assertion of a flame
and daylight, dragged on with my clothes.

II
Sun has saddled up the square
and rides to music

shovelled from a drop-side truck.
Livestock gathers limp rosettes and stares

past oddment-stalls and fancy-dress
to where the river slackens speed

and tadpole parliaments
debate a subtlety of tiny points.

But we have chosen kerb-side vetch
and blue-as-beetroot columbines.

III
Simplified by dusk
we lock our door

on darkness and a sheep-wracked hill.
Closeness joins us at the edge of sleep

and urgency, until dismissed to picnic-fields
where doves combine in crimson blooms

or villages
where suns as delicate as scythes

turn cartwheels in a hive of streets
and interlock their eyes.

Graffiti Maker

Anonymous—a half-seen fist,
an aerosol,
meshed by day-glo traceries—
he spills his culture through the underpass:
represents unpalatable words
and those used only once, then thrown away.

His head is blown with messages,
and all the broadcasts of the gutters
flutter to his feet.
The news looks bleak for sentences:
words are mustering in gangs.
Syllables are swaggering the streets.

Tyneside Boozers

Wreckers comb the back-street rows.
Idle cranes and gantreys nose
the under-arms of sweaty skies,
spitting light into the sties
of half a hundred snoring sows
tethered to their breweries.

Little ones are at the nipple:
Clive who shakes unless he tipples,
Monty with the pornographs.
Somewhere a brewery accountant laughs.
These monsters eat their crippled
litters, waiting till their heads are daft.

Still unweaned and far from pretty—
drinkers in a drinking city—
piss investigates their thighs.
They need to spike their mother's eyes,
aim a boot at each fat titty.
Heaven help them otherwise.

Oil At Tynemouth

With a lure of tide the Port of Tyne
begins to captivate its ships:
a pilot-boat, a ferry on the Norway run.

I search them with a schoolboy's eyes
as through a toyshop telescope:
the slow complexities of portholes

ramps and ducts, anchors fettered in their caves
the weighty rummaging, shifting
of the river's skin. More are brimming in:

tankers off past Sharpness Point
trawlers, pressing to the pier light.
But which of them side-swiped that oily gash

beneath the headland's chin?
Disenchantment snags my throat:
the seas has seen two murders done.

Good Old Snow

You know snow, the drunk who overstays
the party: those mushy monologues,
hogging the conversation of the street.
Then the last collapse, unbudgeable,
between the gaps where cars have sprawled
and oiled themselves through Boxing Day.
Remember how he leans unsteadily
against the roofs: those sudden deluges,
such tasteless jokes, and all at the expense
of grit-stained dog-shat footpaths,
trying to hold down an honest job.
We're glad to see the last of him, and yet

when winter brings the Christmas feast
we'll greet the necessary dishes,
and hope for snow, the welcome guest,
as bright and urgent as our wishes.

Disturbing Deer

Unfit at forty, lightly shod,
we should have set off earlier.
Shadows had already closed
the gap from which we saved a lamb
one Easter, quietly resigned.
The last excitement of the sky
burned out, and underneath the packman's bridge
the beck poured black as Guinness,
froth capsizing wickedly.

Still joking where the Wanney Crags,
holding rock above our heads,
standing nursing their concavity:
but silent as the rain began
and leaned on us as darkness did.
Walking was a clueless stumble
deeper into self-reproach:
the whole embroiling hopeless moor
thrashing our perversity.

Later on we could discern
a remedy for middle age:
set out late and unprepared,
take the hard way, lose the track,
get hunker-deep and soaking wet,
and after blundering enough
disturb a clutch of hurdling deer,
their scuts like marsh-fire flickering,
to prick the torpor, point the rising ground.

Poet Hadrian

Good dry-stone builders make a pact:
though gales barge in,
and frost has access to the core,
unmortared bloodymindedness
can stand intact
its century and even more
before the next sequential sprawl
to recombine and rise again.

But not poor poet Hadrian:
each bonded stone along his wall
became a pledge to Terminus.

Buying Dermott's Shoes

This business of the shoes
is altogether Dermott: oxblood barges
knocked down in the sales, but only he
would buy a pair so overblown
then paddle round in agony
among an archipelago of blisters.

He's known for lack of grip on life:
that awful slum
he lives in, with the kicked-in doors,
the strange neglected wife
in County Cork, the problem-child
who visits for a fortnight every year
by order of the court.

Such shiftlessness defies all remedy:
he'll regularly sleep till noon
then sink the fag-end of the day
adrift among his paperbacks on witchery.
One problem is that our indulgences
cement his inefficiency.
His undernourished grin begins to function
like a honed and balanced tool
with which to lever up the lid of charity.

He plays both mariner and albatross:
a glance from him
can wake the Celtic bogles,
blight the simplest plans to stark confusion.
If you invite him home he'll drink
your booze all night, expound
the paranormal through the early hours,
then slump asleep across a chair
or mumble up and down the house
long after you and yours are in your beds.

It is important to be firm with Dermott,
for his and everybody's good.
Diffuse the focus of that pointed charm:
it is no fault of yours that he is broke again.
Besides, he could be selling more than shoes:
take care, don't even try them on.

Ballad-Plaid

These border fells are cold enough
to freeze the balls off poetry.
Out before me in the snow
has gone James Armstrong, balladeer,
thinly wrapped in sentiment:
startling gorcocks seemingly,
or wrestling with shepherd lads
upon the hills o'Wanny.

That man, untrousered in the wind,
was built of Ridsdale iron.
He left me a stew of doggerel,
warming on the cottage stove,
a name for nowhere and a tune
to whistle while I trace his steps.
But I wear more than ballad-plaid
to fetch the blossoms home.

* James Armstrong of Ridsdale was the author of *Wanny Blossoms*, a collection of
ballad poems and notes on country life published in 1879. His masterpiece
'Wild Hills o'Wannys' is still sung to the Northumbrian Pipes, and was
probably the origin of the phrase 'wilds o'Wanny' which means nowhere.
Gorcocks are the males of the Red Grouse.